How to set up and run a Dementia Memory Cafe

Sandra Hastings

Sandra Hastings

ISBN: 197775984X
ISBN-13: 9781977759849

Sandra Hastings

DEDICATION

This book is dedicated to everyone at Silverline Memories.
The Trustees, Staff and Volunteers who make it all
happen, and to everyone who attends our Café groups
now, in the past, and in the future.

Love is what makes a family, and we are a family.

Sandra Hastings

Sandra Hastings

CONTENTS

Acknowledgments

Foreword by Norrms McNamara

Sandra Hastings

ACKNOWLEDGMENTS

My heartfelt thanks to go to those who have supported
and encouraged me in this writing project. To Tracey Tait
who first suggested it and to Norrms McNamara for his
kind words and advice. To my family for their
unconditional love, especially my mum & step-dad Anne
& Bill, partner James and children Hannah & Matthew and
my big hairy yellow dog Max.

To all the Purple Angels around the globe who were so
enthusiastic when I first suggested this project.

And thank YOU for reading this. You have picked this
book up because you want to make a difference, and that
is priceless. Together we can change the world.

FOREWORD

Hello. My name is Norrms Mc Namara and i am the founder of the Global Purple Angel dementia awareness campaign website https://www.purpleangel-global.com/

I was also diagnosed with dementia myself 10 years ago.

It would take me another book to explain why memory cafes WORK, and WORK they do but here are a few reasons why this book should be read, adhered to and implemented. Quite simply, I have stood and watched people COME ALIVE within themselves whilst attending a memory cafe, and especially whilst music is being played. It really is a wonderful thing when a family member brings along those who are very reserved, very withdrawn and within a couple of weeks they are up dancing, singing and even sometimes playing instruments they used to play before the illness struck. Two words always to remember at you memory cafe is INCLUSION AND ENGAGEMENT . Always keep these in mind and you will have a happy cafe. It's sometimes the simplest of things that give pleasure, I always say when people come week after week and say HI NORRMS, then its job done !! Why ? Because they have remembered my name !!

The memory cafe should be there for all, and please remember, it's their cafe, not yours, you are just the facilitators.

I could not close without saying a HUGE thank you to my great friend Sandra Hastings, Author of this book, who has worked so hard in the field of dementia and strives every day to improve the lives of others

Best wishes, Norrms Mc Namara

1 INTRODUCTION

This is the guide I wish I had been able to find when starting my first Cafe. There was plenty of advice on activities for people with dementia (although I am not sure how many of them had been written by people with dementia or had even included someone with dementia in the research, but that's another story for another time). Everything in this guide has been learned through trial and error, asking questions and simply doing. Mistakes have fortunately been few and none serious, most hilarious at the time and have resulted in a good story to tell. Everything in here is factual and all advice given here has acquired firstly through research and practice.
Before I begin with the practicalities of setting up a Cafe for people living with dementia, please don't ever get bogged down by the diagnosis. Yes, it is the reason you are creating this group. But the service is not for Dementia, it is not about Dementia and the Dementia is not at the centre of what you do. You are there for the people. The fabulous, diverse group of people who just happen to also have a dementia diagnosis. I have met some truly remarkable people, people who I would never have had the privilege to meet were it not for their diagnosis, yet the diagnosis is the very least of who they are. Enjoy their company, rejoice in the life that is to be lived despite any health concerns. Nothing about running a Cafe is hard - yes there is lots to do but all you are really doing is facilitating social opportunities. You provide the space and the place and the rest will follow. Have fun with it, bring joy to the room and the rest will follow. Use this

guide to keep you on the right track, but the rest is up to you.

Sandra x

2 GOVERNANCE

It is not necessary to have a fully developed set of rules, or constitution, before you start, but it is advisable to have a good idea about the purpose and aims of your group and how you want things to run. Once your group is up and running and things are settling into a routine then you ought to consider what legal structure is best suited to the aims of your organisation. Try not to get too bogged down with the options during the early stages especially, go for the simplest option for your group at the time. You can always "upgrade" later

OPTION	PROS	CONS
Unincorporated Association	Simplest option Quick and easy to set up Fewest regulations No external reporting is required	Limited funding options The group will have no separate legal identity so members of the Committee are personally liable for any debts, including any legal action taken against the group Not able to claim Gift Aid on donations

Charitable Unincorporated Association	As above; plus: Additional funding options are available Gift Aid available.	If your income exceeds £5000 you must register with the Charities Commission You must be able demonstrate in your constitution that the group has charitable aims
Charitable Incorporated Organisation	Wide range of funding options Limited personal liability Trustees	Full annual accounts must be prepared by a firm of accountants An annual report must be submitted to the Charities Commission that include your signed annual accounts Longer and more complex process to register.

3 INSURANCE

At the very least you will need public liability insurance before starting your group and if you have volunteers at the group then you will also need employers liability. Some venues specify the amount of cover required before allowing you to hire space from them. Find a specialist insurance broker for community groups/charities. From experience using a High Street broker or comparison site results in much higher premiums than is necessary. Finding a company who has a true understanding of the third sector leads to a longer lasting relationship and someone you can call as your service develops to ensure you have the right cover in place.

Insurance companies also like to know you have carried out Risk Assessments for your venues. There are lots of websites that can guide you in completing one but the most effective use a scale that reflects the impact of an event occurring versus the likelihood of that event occurring. So for example, a fire could have a catastrophic impact on your group, but the likelihood of it happening is low enough for it not to cause a huge concern, especially if normal precautions are taken such as having access to a fire extinguisher.

4 TRAINING

Training is a funny one. On one hand there can be no doubt that finding the right person is so much more important than finding someone with the right qualifications. The right person can always be taught any skills they may be missing, but it is virtually impossible to teach anyone how to have the right qualities for a role within a Dementia Cafe environment. However, no matter how much personal and/or professional experience someone has, for your own peace of mind in the quality of the service you're providing, the minimum training provided should include:

- Dementia Awareness
- Safeguarding Vulnerable Adults
- Person Centred Care
- Food Hygiene Certificate
- Emergency First Aid at Work

You may also want to consider Managing Challenging Behaviour should you recognise a need for this among those who attend your group. This may be something that is not needed initially, but when the group has been running a while and the needs of those attending develop at a pace consistent with their diagnosis.

Over time you will recognise additional training needs. For example, if you spot a volunteer who likes a bit of a natter (polite term for gossip!), you might choose to add in some Confidentiality training but remember to include ALL volunteers so as not to single anyone out and cause offence!

5 FUNDING

Funding any kind of start-up is a minefield and unless you plan to charge a likely prohibitive amount in the early days at least you are going to juggling or using your own funds to start you off. Look for free venues, free community rooms, church halls etc you can use. Keep the costs low. Many supermarkets and bakeries will offer donations of tea, coffee & biscuits so you only have fresh milk to buy. Most speakers are willing to give their time for free and many activities can be planned at minimal cost. Do request a donation though - and remember that by asking for a donation as opposed to charging a fee, you can claim back Gift Aid when/if you take on a legal charitable status.

Grant funding is a very good idea, even in the early stages but be aware that many funders will only grant awards to those groups with clearly defined charitable aims. Funding advice is readily available to community groups. Different funders have different requirements so be careful to read the guidelines carefully. Applications can appear very daunting at first but as you become familiar with making applications you will recognise a pattern to the questions that in time you can have prepared responses for (although don't forget to tailor your responses to the funder, much as you would do when applying for jobs). As a general rule funders require the following:

- Evidence of need
- Evidence that your proposal will meet that need
- How you will prove that it has worked

In addition most will ask you to state what the outcomes of your project will be and they want them to follow the SMART rule:

- S - Specific. What will happen?
- M - Measurable. How many? How much?
- A - Achievable. Is it realistic? How will it happen?
- R - Realistic. Don't overstate.
- T - Time. By when? How long?

Most funders will also require a copy of your constitution and for your group to have a bank account in the name of the group. Most will also need for your bank account to require two signatures for cheques so it is recommended that you have three people authorised for your account with any two able to sign.

Funders are just people and from experience are very approachable. They want to help - they have the money and want to give it to projects who can make the most difference with it. Funders are experienced and know what can be achieved with what amount of money and in what timescale. They understand that often your idea is brilliant but you just need help in wording the application to properly demonstrate the sheer genius of your idea. Ring them.

6 STARTING OUT - WHAT'S IN A NAME?

Finding the right name for your organisation can be one of the trickiest aspects of starting any new venture, much like naming a new baby! The name is going to be around for a long time (hopefully). Consider how it may be shortened or any acronyms it may be associated with. Another thing to consider is how you describe the group. Is it Memory Cafe or a Dementia Cafe? Some prefer Memory Cafe, feeling this to be a more positive position than using the term Dementia. Others use Dementia Cafe as a way of raising awareness or busting the myths that everything about Dementia is negative. Others choose neither and instead a generic name such as Rainbow Cafe, or Butterfly Cafe (although there are sure to be Cafes with these names, these have been chosen as random examples and are not an advert for any groups using these names. (Phew).   A good test for any name is to check it out on the internet. Is there already a group/organisation using that name? Is there a domain name free should you decide to build a website for your group? It may also be wise to check on Companies House and the Charity Commission. Ask family and friends what comes to mind when they hear the name.

7 FINDING A VENUE

The venue for your cafe is so important. As well as checking availability for a regular, long term booking and the cost of hiring the space, you must consider accessibility of both the building and toilet facilities, but also location. Can it be easily accessed by public transport? Is it somewhere where local people may also benefit from the activities available? Is there parking? Is there a kitchen available to you, ideally with a hatch into the space you will be holding the group. Is it the right size - big enough to accommodate the group including any wheelchairs/walking frames they may require, but not so big as to feel cavernous and without atmosphere. Consider decor also - spaces with very busy wallpaper or carpets can be disorientating for those with specific dementia types and lots of mirrors may also cause challenges that may spoil the experience for those attending.

8 YOUR TEAM

When starting a new group, it is very likely that the group will be run by people you already know, family and friends. You'll be calling on people you know you can trust and rely on to support your idea in the early stages. This kind of help is invaluable. However, no matter how well you may know someone you must not lose sight of the fact that you are going to working with adults who in law are classed as vulnerable, and to prove that you are safeguarding their welfare whilst attending your group it is important that everyone involved (including yourself) is subject to a DBS check. The Disclosure and Barring Service replaced the Criminal Records Bureau and is the method used to ensure that everyone involved in the organisation has no Police convictions that would prevent them from working with vulnerable adults. There are several ways to obtain a DBS for an individual, including using an umbrella organisation, or registering your own organisation with a company that can carry out the checks on your behalf. There is a cost per check but this does tend to be less for volunteer roles.

When the time comes to add to your team consider carefully the type of person you want and what role you need him/her to fulfil. Be very clear in your role description what is required and what qualities you are looking for. Don't dismiss those without well written applications - remember you are looking for specific qualities that can exist without impressive qualifications. From experience it is recommended that at a minimum you seek people who have personal or professional experience of dementia, personal being so much more valuable than professional. Although everyone's experience is as unique as the individual living it, lived experience of supporting someone with dementia gives an insight that books and training never can.

Always, always take up references and provide an on-boarding programme, giving any applicant a feel for the very heart of your organisation. And always offer a probationary period and trust your gut. If you don't feel that they are really "getting" your group, then end the relationship during the probation period. Your group is only as good as the people delivering it and you have so much more than the reputation of your organisation to safeguard.

9 ADVERTISING

In the early stages you will want and need to make as much noise about your group as you can. Make a simple poster to display in your chosen venue and local shops and libraries. GP surgeries tend only to display posters of registered charities (frustrating but understandable) but it is worth asking as it is at the discretion of the Practice Manager. Use social media. A lot. Create a Page for your group on Facebook to share details of your plans and promote the group times. Create a Twitter ID and get very comfortable with spending your evenings chatting to strangers in sentences of 140 characters or less. With Twitter especially, you only get out of Social Media what you put into it. Build relationships, let people get to know you so that if they hear of someone living with dementia you are who they think of. Let the word get out that way. Avoid repetitive "selling" tweets. You will end up with no followers and no-one reading about the fantastic work you are doing.

Websites are a great idea but start simply and remember they are living things that need to be updated. If you change the time or venue or add a new service it is important you keep the site updated to reflect what you offer. Consider a web chat service also so that visitors to your site can have simple questions answered immediately without having to make a call or send an email. Share your website content onto your social media platforms to drive traffic back to your website. In the very early days though don't worry too much about a website - even those using a search engine will see results from a Facebook Page and can visit your page. It is the cheapest way to build an audience and the simplest to keep your followers updated when starting out.

10 TAKING REFERRALS

Unless you are looking at taking commissioned funds then you don't necessarily have to limit the geographic boundaries from which you will accept referrals. However, depending on the size of your venue and the demand for your group you may choose to limit the group by location, so only serve people living in a particular area or region. Referrals may come in to you from a range of sources from individuals themselves, friends, families, health and social care professionals and may be taken by whatever means you choose - written, telephone, email, face to face. It is always wise though to collect a certain amount of basic information regarding the person being referred, for insurance and peace of mind purposes. At a minimum consider collecting the following data:

- Full Name and preferred name (Betty for Elizabeth as an example)
- Date of Birth (useful for lots of reasons, not least so you can celebrate birthdays)
- Contact information - address, telephone numbers, email address
- Alternative contact. It is sometimes necessary to send letters/emails to a family member and not the person being referred to your service
- Any relevant medical information. As well as the dementia diagnosis, is there anything else you need to know? For example is the person diabetic or epileptic? Consider also collecting this information from anyone attending the Cafe with the person with

the diagnosis - medical emergencies can happen to anyone and the more information you can pass to the emergency services the better.

- Hobbies/interests. This is SO important. The individual may not be able to communicate the things they enjoy doing or what his/her hobbies were prior to a diagnosis, but the more you know the better you can plan group activities to make that person feel welcome and engaged in the Cafe.

- Consent - to photos being taken; to photos being shared for marketing purposes.

- Data Protection statement. It may seem overkill but registering your group with the Information Commissioners Office provides reassurance to those sharing their data with you that it will be stored safely and securely, but it also provides you with guidance on your duties towards that data and advice on data protection.

11 RECORD KEEPING

Record keeping is unfortunately a necessary evil. Not only will it provide you with information useful both for the management of your group and as evidence of your service for funders, but it is also arguably one of the most important safeguards your Cafe has. An accident book is essential, although this is one record it is hoped it rarely, if ever, used. Financial records are also essential, (subs paid, donations made, etc), but it is also important to have some anecdotal record of each session you deliver. Things to record include:

- Who attended
- Which volunteers were present
- Any visitors to the group
- Anything significant that occurred?
- Any Safeguarding concerns? This is a HUGE one and as such deserves its own chapter

12 SAFEGUARDING

Sharing concerns you have about the welfare of someone attending your Cafe is a legal responsibility that falls under Duty of Care. At the most basic level it also protects your group against any future action - should you suspect something and not act then you must also accept some responsibility should any significant harm later befall the person you had concerns about. It is advisable to appoint someone within your group as Safeguarding Officer, and ensure that they have attended full training, beyond the basic training the rest of your volunteers may have attended. They must be fully aware of the process to follow in the event they have their own concern and what to do if a concern is brought to them by someone else. You must also make all your volunteers aware of who the Safeguarding Officer is and how to contact him/her. It may not always be appropriate or convenient for a concern to be reported during a Cafe session but a concern must always be reported as soon as it practically possible. For this reason the Safeguarding Officer must be contactable outside of Cafe times and be willing to be disturbed for this purpose.

13 CONFIDENTIALITY

It should go without saying that everyone attending your Cafe, and those who volunteer, are entitled to confidentiality and privacy. Conversations should never the leave the room (unless there is a safeguarding concern as above, then you have a duty to disclose something you hear, even if in told confidence). Your group members should feel able to talk freely and openly without being the subject of conversation beside the coffee machine. They should know their data is stored safely in accordance with Data Protection regulations. If using an individual as a case study for a funding application always ask for permission while reassuring that no names will be used, only initials and even those do not have to be factual.

 It is inevitable that at times something will happen during the course of a Cafe that you would not normally expect to happen somewhere else. Dementia brings with it behaviour that can shock or challenge. A loss of inhibition is common and sexualised behaviour/comments etc can happen on a somewhat regular basis. If someone is easily offended, shocked or likely to create a fuss if someone pinches or pats their bottom as they walk past then you may consider whether they would be the right volunteer for your group. Obviously you have a responsibility to safeguard your team as much as those attending the group and you may need to put measures in place occasionally to ensure the safety of everyone attending. As you get to know your group members you will know those who it is unwise to hug when they come in, or when to ensure there is never a one to one situation with a member of the opposite sex. Whatever the situation, given human nature it is inevitable that situations like this will be top of the list of things to mention when people ask member of the team "how was your day?". And this is the point where confidentiality training must kick in. It is absolutely reasonable that if something shocking or upsetting has happened that there is need to "offload", but is also essential that details are kept to an absolute minimum so that the individual involved cannot be identified from anything that is shared. So saying "I had my bum pinched today" is ok, saying who did the pinching is not. Nor is chatting about anything at all in a public place, and especially not if others in the area may recognise you from an ID badge or uniform. It is so true when people say that walls have ears. It is also important to consider how that individual would feel if they were not unwell? Any one of us could develop dementia in the future and who is say how we may behave. How would we feel if our actions were the subject of gossip?

As a group leader you do have a responsibility to your team to give them the opportunity to offload any concerns/fears in a safe environment and to provide any support they may require longer term. However, for those who just enjoy juicy tidbit, it may be worth considering their future with your organisation and making it clear just why they are not the right person to be supporting your Cafe.

14 PHOTOS

Photos are fantastic and an absolutely brilliant way to record the activities that take place during your Cafe sessions. Not only is it a visual record of the sessions but sharing physical copies of the photos with the group members is a great way of sharing memories. Photos are often requested by funders seeking evidence of your work and as a way of demonstrating the joy your group brings. It is very difficult to demonstrate to funders the power of a smile from someone who in non-verbal in any other way that in a photo. Take as many pictures as you can and share them in as many ways as possible - *as long as you have permission of the people in them!* Some people may be happy to have their photo taken so long as it is not shared publically. That's absolutely fine, take as many photos of them as you would everyone else but print them for the group album and that way they stay in the room.

15 TELLING THE WORLD

You are doing amazing work. You are making a difference to those people who need it most. So tell everyone. Shout about it from the roof tops. Not to brag, not for personal recognition (very few people are genuinely comfortable with "bigging" themselves up and those who are not necessarily the kind of people you'd want to invite round for dinner), but so that you can reach those who need you but have not yet heard of you. Nothing is harder than someone joining your group and telling you how they wish they knew about you earlier, especially when you have been running for more than two years. That hurts because you know what they have been going through and how much your group could have helped, but you couldn't because you hadn't reached them. The best way to reach people is to shout about what you do. Use social media, share photos, share feedback, share videos of people dancing at your groups, singing, smiling, laughing - whatever it is share it. If you can get people to let you video them for just 30 seconds stating what your Cafe means to them then do just that. Video is so much more powerful that just words or even still photos. Send out press releases. Unless you are lucky enough to have a marketing budget then getting the word out about your group is down to you and the time you are willing to put into it. Join in hashtag hours on Twitter, talk to people at bus stops. Wear T-Shirts with your Cafe name on, sign write your vehicle - whatever you can do to let people know you are there and can help, do it.

16 DEVELOPING YOUR SERVICE (OFFERING A LITTLE BIT MORE)

When our own group started in May 2014, there was no vision for how it looks today. It was expected to be a group that would offer a monthly opportunity for people living with dementia to get together over a cuppa for a chat. It was a home based organisation with minimal governance and three people involved in its birth. Almost four years later and now a Charitable Incorporated Organisation with a Board of Trustees, Staff and Volunteers delivering an average of twenty social opportunity per calendar month, it is hard to even track the journey of how we came to be where we are today. What is clear to all though is that the group developed because we listened. We listened to the needs of our group members in the first instance, and then to their wants, and where it was in our power to meet those needs and wants, we did our very best to do so. Not everything we tried worked. Some things we were asked for and offered and then they weren't wanted any longer and that was ok. We exist for our group members and not the other way around. Some services we tried that were very popular among the very few who attended and tough decisions had to be made. We're still too young an organisation to take financial risks and once a fund has gone, it has gone. Very few people won't understand that, especially when the option is the end of one service short term or the end of the organisation in the longer term.

17 LISTEN, LISTEN, AND LISTEN SOME MORE

As with the activities you offer, it is so, so important to listen to your group members. What do they chat about? What issues are they dealing with? If you realise the group are dealing with a specific issue and you can help, then offer that help. This may be as simple as arranging for someone to come in to the group to talk them about a specific issue. As an example, male carers may be heard talking about the challenges their partners are experiencing with applying make-up - so bring in a make-up artist to talk to the whole group with demonstrations. Another example may be advice on foot care - bring in a Chiropodist to do a fun and informative talk. Dementia brings all kinds of challenges but they don't all have to be addressed in a serious or even an obvious way. Some subjects however are sensitive and consideration must always be given to how these issues are addressed so as not to cause embarrassment or discomfort, especially when creating an environment that people come to "leave dementia at the door". This is where you may consider creating a separate Carers Group who can meet for an hour once or twice a month at the same time as the main Cafe group. During this time you can arrange for experts to come in to give advice on matters such as Continence or Nutrition, or on legal matters such as Power of Attorney. Don't forget that there will be those living with a diagnosis who also want to be present at these talks and that should never be discouraged, but equally there are those who would find certain subjects uncomfortable and equally they should have the option to not be there.

By listening to your group and understanding their needs, both as individuals and collectively, you will come to recognise the things you can do to help and in this way the service you offer will be develop organically. Don't force change or development - remember you are there to meet the needs of those who attend your group, and not the other way around.

18 TRIAL AND ERROR

Don't be disheartened when you offer a new service or activity and it does not prove popular. You are working with a group of individuals, all with their own likes and dislikes, wants and desires. There will be those who love Arts & Crafts and those who hate it. Those who love a game of Dominoes or Bingo, and those who would rather stick pins in their eyes! As the saying goes, you can't please all of the people all of the time - but what you can do is pay attention. What works well, what engages people. If possible have a back-up plan so that if a group activity is not going as planned, you have something else to fall back on. Even something as simple as having someone nip out on a hot day to bring back ice lollies for everyone can be enough to make the break from a disastrous activity to a lovely interval during the session! And please don't ever feel that you have to "entertain" for every minute of your group session. Often all people need is chat with their friends to feel like they have had a smashing afternoon out. All you need to do is offer the right environment and, given time, your group will develop its own heartbeat.

19 OVER TO YOU

Experience has shown that a successful Cafe is nothing less than a family. A group of people, all individual with unique likes and dislikes and hopes and fears. All united by an unwanted diagnosis yet learning, with your help, that there is still so much life to be lived and joy to be found, if someone just creates the opportunity for it to be found. Someone like you.

Good Luck.

20 FURTHER ADVICE AND TRAINING

Details of further advice and training available by the author is available at www.TheBigD.online. Sign up for updates.

ABOUT THE AUTHOR

Sandra Hastings is the Founder & Chief Operating Officer of Silverline Memories, a charity that provides "Places to go and things to do" for people living with Dementia. She lives in Newcastle upon Tyne.

For more information about Silverline Memories please visit

www.silverlinememories.com